FOR HUNGRY CATS EVERYWHERE,
hoping they get a tasty treat.

MEOW CHOW

HEARTY RECIPES
for HAPPY CATS

Julia Szabo

Photographs by Jonathon Kambouris
AND JULIA SZABO

CONTENTS

PUSHKIN

THE AMERICAN BLUE
IS THE PICTURE OF
LICK-YOUR-CHOPS
DELECTATION.
GIVE THAT CAT
A SNACK!

INTrODUCTION

If you fancy yourself a gourmet, then the cat is your ideal pet. Everyone knows the stereotype of the finicky feline. Well, this is one stereotype that's right on target: Cats are notoriously discerning about what they eat. However, while you are a gourmet, your cat is a grrr-met. House cats are essentially parlor-size tigers, and they share many characteristics with their majestic, wild counterparts.

Unlike dogs, who are opportunistic omnivores (they can survive by eating just about anything), cats, big and small, are serious carnivores: they love meat. Not only do they love it, they live or die by it. Cats are obligate carnivores, which means they absolutely must have meat to survive. Although some cats will eat vegetables on occasion, there is no such thing as a vegetarian cat. (And while the occasional carbohydrate is OK as a treat, felines' carb intake should be kept to a minimum, to lower the risk of diabetes and cancer.)

These are animals with very high standards, and they are equally uncompromising about the "tableware" they eat and drink from. If made of cheap plastic, a bowl imparts a taste to water that's off-putting to cats. For some cats, water in a bowl is simply not fresh enough; they will reject water bowls completely, preferring to drink fresh water only from a steady drip in the faucet.

Cats also love creamy things. Most of us can recall in our mind's eye the archetypal image of the kitten lapping at a saucer of cream. Although we've since learned that milk and cream are not the healthiest dietary options for cats, there are many other creamy things they can enjoy safely from time to time, in moderation, including small amounts of butter (an excellent remedy for hairballs) and yogurt. One cat I know loves organic cashew butter!

My cats do very well in the spontaneous treat department, for I find myself powerless to resist their sweet little faces, urgent pawing, and insistent meow-meow-meows. They eat pretty much everything I do—unless, of course, I'm indulging in what no cat should ever eat, i.e., anything containing onions, grapes, raisins, chocolate, or extremely spicy, salty, or sweet foods.

Indeed, if I wish to get a bite in edgewise—especially when the meal or snack in question involves scrambled eggs, roasted meat, or any kind of salmon, cooked or uncooked—I must temporarily close my cats out of my kitchen, or I don't stand a chance!

Some people believe that cats should eat a strict diet of pre-packaged cat food. And yet, before cat food was mass-produced, sharing "people" food with cats was the only option. Traditionally, cats were not strangers to the kitchen or pantry. In ancient Egypt, the feline became a deity because he protected valuable grain from the depredations of rodents. Today, a very popular purveyor of bread in New York City goes by the handle Tom Cat Bakery. These days, our busy schedules make catering special cat-meals inconvenient—especially if, like me, you have more than one cat. Besides, prepared cat foods contain certain vitamins and minerals (notably Taurine) that our feline friends require for optimal well-being.

As this book will prove, you needn't toss out your cat's preferred canned food to become a full-time chef. There are simple, creative ways to enhance the flavor of feline food, enabling Kitty to share in your feasts without harming her or inconveniencing yourself.

A heart-shaped dish is one way to tell a cat "I love you."

More than a strict recipe book, *Meow Chow* is a lifestyle guide to enhancing everyday meals for the four—and two—legged. However, there are some cats (and people) who cannot eat certain foods or they risk serious illness. Cats who suffer from allergies and are prescribed specific diets by their veterinarians must stick with that diet without deviation, or they risk an allergic reaction that, at its worst, could result in death. (Luckily for these animals, there's Purina HA, a highly palatable hypoallergenic diet.) But for the rest, there is this book. Let the recipes and recommendations on these pages help you share every meal with your feline friend—for their pleasure and yours. Enjoy!

Where dogs are gourmands, cats are serious gourmets. Discerning and elegant, they don't eat just anything. This is how they got their well-earned reputation for being "finicky."

Cats are enormously entertaining to observe as they eat; their focused, primal munching recalls the concentrated intensity of tigers devouring the kill.

Felines eat efficiently, and when they've had their fill, they don't stoop to lick the plate clean (how canine and gauche!). Like Curly Sue the Cornish Rex, they have the good taste to walk away

private DINING

If you share your home with dogs as well as cats, you've doubtless observed how the canines are always trying to steal the felines' food. That's because cat food is higher in protein. Cats are obligate carnivores, so they absolutely must eat meat or they die. Dogs, on the other hand, are opportunistic omnivores—although meat is high on their list of favorite foods, they can survive by eating pretty much anything, from vegetables to oats.

In a multi-species household, dogs will be dogs, constantly on the prowl for cat food. That's why it's important to provide Fluffy with a safe, secure place well out of Fido's reach—especially if freshly cooked meat is on the *Meow Chow* menu.

Cats are arboreal creatures, which means they instinctively feel safe up high, as in trees. It's a good idea to build an indoor "branch": a shelf like this one.

Make sure to place the shelf near a piece of furniture (such as a chair or end table) that doubles as the cat's launch pad, and install it well out of Fido's reach so Kitty can savor her dinner in peace. Her very own dedicated dining nook will also provide your cat the privacy she needs to follow her meal with a thorough "washing" session (fastidious creatures, felines enjoy cleaning themselves after every meal).

Provide Fluffy with three or more cat shelves arranged decoratively along the wall, and she'll also enjoy staying in shape—not to mention working off *Meow Chow* calories!—by jumping from "branch" to "branch."

In a multi-species household, this Fiesta bowl says it all!

move over rover

kitty's taking over

GOURMET CAT TREATS
ARE AN EXCELLENT WAY
TO COAX A CAT TO POSE
FOR THE CAMERA, AS
HANNAH
DEMONSTRATES.

BreakFast

Yogurt

· · · · · · · · ·

Scrambled Eggs with Kefir

· · · · · · · · ·

Soft-boiled Eggs

· · · · · · · · ·

Amelia Jane's Tuna and Mash

· · · · · · · · ·

Sardines

crème De La crème

Cats love foods with a creamy texture. They will even salivate at the prospect of non-edible creaminess, such as hand cream, which is why I take care to use only all-natural, organic beauty products that contain nothing harmful—for those times when my cats diligently lick the cream off my hands as I drift off to sleep.

Most creamy-textured edibles contain dairy, and despite the archetypal image of the cat with the saucer of cream, dairy products are not a staple of the feline diet. "Cats are like lactose-intolerant people," explains Dr. Heather Peikes of Animal Allergy and Dermatology Specialists in New York City. "They lack the enzyme needed to break down milk, and can get diarrhea if they ingest milk in large amounts."

However, in moderation, most cats can tolerate yogurt, so if you're having yogurt with your morning cereal or fruit, do offer Kitty a teaspoon.

CANDY

THE SIAMESE
ENJOYS THE CREAMY
TEXTURE OF PLAIN
YOGURT.

TIP:

Feel free to share an eggy breakfast treat with
your favorite feline. If you know your eggs are
free-range and super-fresh, you can even
serve the yolk raw.

FELINE EGG-CENTRICS

Cat lovers are early risers—but not always by choice. At dawn, the time when my insistent cats like to waken me for feeding, I'm sometimes too tired to do much more than open a can of cat food and stumble back into bed. But if I need to stay awake, it's fun to get a jump on the day by sharing eggs with my hungry felines.

Eggs have the texture cats love and the protein they crave (plus beneficial vitamin D and Biotin, a B vitamin). The occasional raw-egg treat is OK, as long as you're certain that the eggs you're serving are organic and very, very fresh. If there's any doubt, play it safe by boiling the egg for 2 minutes and 15 seconds, then running under cold water to cool.

A high-protein breakfast benefits everyone, two- and four-legged, especially on a cold winter morning. So why not make scrambled eggs even richer in protein by adding something extra? An excellent source of acidophilus, Kefir is a wonderful type of liquid yogurt that's full of other active cultures to help maintain healthy intestinal flora. Plus, it makes for creamier, fluffier eggs—a meal that combines two of Kitty's favorite things: eggs and cream.

scrambled eggs with kefir

———— ►■◄ ————

2 eggs
1 teaspoon Kefir

Olive oil for misting

Using a wire whisk, beat eggs until frothy; add Kefir. Use an oil mister to spray a small amount of olive oil into a cast-iron pan. Heat over medium flame. Pour in egg-kefir mixture; allow to set, about 1 minute, then swirl edges toward center; allow to set again for about 1 minute. Do not overcook—the looser and creamier, the better. Turn off heat, let Kitty's portion cool, and serve.

SERVES ONE PERSON (1 ½ EGGS) AND ONE CAT (½ EGG)

Use a mortar and pestle to break the eggshell into bite-size bits before serving.

SOFT-BOILED EGGS

Everyone loves eggs. They are a wonderful way to supplement a cat's meal, especially in the cold of winter, when everyone likes to feel warm and fortified. According to the Egg Nutrition Center, at the time of the French Revolution, French foodies had already mastered no fewer than 685 ways of preparing eggs—including, of course, the omelet. For a simpler egg treat, soft-boil an egg and serve its contents in a bowl, or break it over your cat's kibble. Your feline gourmet will love the way the yolk and white combine to form a rich, kibble-enhancing gravy. She may even like nibbling the egg shell, which is a fine source of calcium—just crush it into small pieces to help her out.

In a small covered pot, place eggs in water over high heat. When water begins to boil, time the eggs for exactly 2 minutes and 15 seconds. Cool the eggs by holding under cold running water. Break and serve over kibble, or spoon into a bowl.

RECOMMENDED SERVING: ½ EGG PER CAT

amelia Jane's tuna and mash

———— ✦ ————

Amelia Jane is a high-maintenance moggy (a Britishism deriving from the Cockney slang for cat). She is named for the titular character in Enid Blyton's delightful Amelia Jane *series of books, about the adventures of a little doll who bosses around all the other toys. The eccentricities of the feline Amelia Jane are humored because she talks—and she has so much to say! Here is her favorite morning meal.*

1 can (6-ounce) tuna, packed
   in olive oil
1 small red or new potato,
   peeled, steamed and
   mashed with a fork

Garlic flakes
Scant teaspoon plain yogurt

Combine the tuna, mashed potato, and a sprinkling of garlic flakes; stir in the yogurt and serve.

NOTE: The pampered Amelia Jane often follows her Tuna and Mash with a palate-cleansing teaspoonful of goat's milk yogurt drizzled with honey!

SERVES ONE LARGE CAT OR TWO SMALL ONES

some like it dry

Even if you can't always prepare fresh meals for your cat, you can enhance any meal quickly and simply by misting with olive oil or stirring in ½ teaspoon of flaxseed oil. After a few weeks, Kitty's coat will grow healthier and noticeably more shiny.

Veterinarians agree that canned cat food is preferable to dry, as kibble is higher in carbohydrates, which can put cats at risk for Diabetes. But if your cat refuses to eat anything but kibble, ensure the freshness of dry cat food by purchasing small bags. After opening, seal the bag tight with low-stick tape (the bright blue kind available at paint-supply stores) and store, along with a metal feed scoop, in a metal container with a tight-fitting lid.

Keep an oil mister handy to moisten dry kibble, especially in winter.

JASMINE

THE FRISKY KITTEN,
ON THE PROWL FOR A
CRUNCHY NIBBLE.

TO MARKET, TO MARKET

When doing your grocery shopping, keep your cat's silver palate in mind, and think of ways to vary his diet with a real-meal treat here or a canned-sardine snack there. (And if you happen to be in an Asian market, pick up some dried bonito flakes: these are an extra-special fishy treat most cats love.) Kitty will appreciate your consideration at mealtime—and later, he'll enjoy nesting in the cardboard delivery box!

Sardines in olive oil make a tasty feline breakfast treat; reserve a few for your own lunch snack later.

LUNCH

Tuna Fish

· · · · · · · ·

Melina's Seafood Salad Sandwiches

· · · · · · · ·

Kitty's Codcakes

· · · · · · · ·

Filtered Water

SOMETHING'S FISHY

Another popular feline stereotype casts the cat as a passionate seafood lover. While most cats do adore fish, and several are known to devour tuna or salmon directly from the can, others simply don't care for it—and some are even allergic to it. "Tuna is so often fed to cats as treats or in their food, that it's quite common to see cats develop an allergy to the tuna," explains Dr. Heather Peikes of Animal Allergy and Dermatology Associates in New York City. Signs that your cat is allergic include gastrointestinal upset (vomiting, diarrhea), runny eyes, and increased scratching, especially about the ears. If you're not certain how your cat will react to fresh or canned fish, try experimenting with different flavors of cat food that contain tuna or salmon. (One brand of food I know even contains fresh-water trout!)

If your cat is OK with tuna, always keep on hand several extra cans—just in case it's the middle of the night, no stores near you are open, and you forgot to buy regular cat food. Here's another tip: If the cupboard is bare of tuna *and* cat food, pick up a tiny jar of plain chicken or beef baby food. This will tide Kitty over until you can stock up on provisions.

CAP'N ANDY

THE CORNISH REX
HAPPENS TO ADORE
TUNA. IF YOUR CAT DOES
TOO, EXTRA CANS COME
IN HANDY IF YOU FIND
YOURSELF OUT OF
CAT FOOD.

Melina's Seafood Salad Sandwiches

Some kids adore tuna; others can't stand it. For those who like it, this recipe is a lunch-box staple—and a safe, fun way for kids to share a bite with a favorite feline.

For finicky kids, be sure to clip off the bread crusts; for a children's-party luncheon, use a cookie cutter to create fish- or cat- shaped tuna sandwiches. To keep things festive at a party, serve the cookie-cutter sandwiches in a ceramic "Here Kitty Kitty" bowl by Fiesta: kids will get a big kick out of it, and if you're feeling generous, you can send each young party guest home with her very own bowl. As for the cat, once she discovers how creamy this tuna salad is, she probably won't be able to resist!

A fish-shaped ceramic plate is very feline-appropriate "tableware."

Melina's Seafood Salad Sandwiches

5 ounces canned tuna, packed in water

1 tablespoon olive oil

1 tablespoon low-fat mayonnaise

About 4 tablespoons peeled and finely grated fresh carrots

4 slices of sourdough, rye, or whole-wheat bread

Combine the ingredients in a medium bowl, mixing until well-blended and creamy. Spread on a slice of bread. Top with another slice to form a sandwich, and press together. If using a cookie cutter to cut out fun-shaped sandwiches, press the bread slices together extra-firmly.

NOTE: Canned salmon may be substituted for the tuna.

MAKES AT LEAST TWO SANDWICHES

KITTY'S CODCAKES

Besides making a great snack for Kitty, this lip-smacking recipe for codfish cakes also makes a fine lunch treat or—if the batter is formed into bite-size balls—hors d'oeuvres for a cocktail party.

1 pound fresh skinless,
  boneless cod fillet
2 tablespoons olive oil
1 large egg, lightly beaten

2 tablespoons mayonnaise
2 tablespoons Dijon mustard
6 tablespoons breadcrumbs
3 tablespoons chopped
  fresh parsley

Preheat the oven to 400°F. Place cod in a baking dish; rub with 1 tablespoon oil. Roast fish in oven until cooked through, about 15 minutes. Let cool completely, then pat dry with paper towels. Flake with a fork.

In a large bowl, combine cod, egg, mayonnaise, mustard, breadcrumbs, and parsley. Mix very gently, until ingredients just bind together. Form mixture into small patties. Heat 1 tablespoon oil in a nonstick pan over medium heat. Cook cakes until golden brown, about 2 minutes on each side.

NOTE: To modify for humans, add salt and freshly ground pepper to the batter. Serve kitty's portion plain; serve humans' portion with tartar sauce.

SERVES FOUR PEOPLE (OR TWO PEOPLE AND TWO CATS, WITH PLENTY OF LEFTOVERS)

clean
and pure

Health-conscious people take care to filter their tap water, especially when filling a child's sippy cup, yet it doesn't always occur to them to do the same for their cats. One of the most important things you can do for your feline friend is to make sure the water she drinks is free of impurities that could harm her, so she's hydrated and healthy. So please provide Kitty with clean, clear water in a ceramic or metal bowl that's washed every day. The Brita filtration system rids water of unwanted chemicals and sediments, and it's convenient and easy on the eyes— especially if we're looking at the collectible pitcher designed by architect Michael Graves.

Make water available to your cat at all times, in a metal bowl that's washed often.

CYRUS

THE PERSIAN MIX
PREFERS FILTERED
WATER—AND YOUR CAT
PROBABLY DOES TOO.
BRITA DOES THE
JOB NICELY.

JACK AND
HIS PERSIAN
CHARLIE
SHARE FILTERED
WATER FROM JACK'S
SIPPY CUP.

Even if their bowls are washed thoroughly with hot water and soap twice daily, and filled to the brim with filtered or bottled water, some cats still prefer to drink directly from the tap. If that's the case, go with the flow and leave one faucet with a slow drip to help Kitty hydrate whenever the spirit moves her.

TIP:

Out of respect for cats' legendary sense of taste, their food bowls must be cleaned with regularity. When washing a cat's bowls, take care to use a gentle, environmentally-friendly product that won't leave behind a foul-tasting residue. And always rinse thoroughly with clean water, no matter what cleaning product is used.

DINNer

---•---

The Hungry Cat's Crab Cakes

·········

Steak au Poivre/Steak au Naturel

·········

Roast Turkey

·········

Tom's Chicken Soup

Felines
and Foodies

What is the powerful connection between felines and foodies? People who are serious about food are usually serious about cats too. The eminent food writer M.F.K. Fisher was a devoted cat lover; so is noted author Ruth Reichl, who says, "As far as I'm concerned cats rank right up there with butter: Life without them is not worth living." Chef Seen Lippert, who has four cats, developed a mouthwatering flourless dessert she calls the "cat torte" (see page 86 for the recipe) when, searching all over her kitchen, she couldn't locate a ring mold and cleverly decided to substitute an empty cat-food tin—of course, she sterilized it first. And Suzanne Goin, the star chef-owner of Los Angeles' fabulous Lucques and AOC Wine Bar, is a self-described "cat fanatic." Together with her husband, chef David Lentz, Suzanne opened a Hollywood eatery called The Hungry Cat.

Yoda and Tweety Bird are the brother-and-sister kitties who inspired the creation of The Hungry Cat. "We got the cats when they were about seven weeks old," Suzanne explains. "A friend of ours found them abandoned behind his apartment building and fed them with a dropper. The vet didn't think they would live. So, maybe because they were abandoned, they are obsessed with food. We have to keep their dry food locked up in the fridge because one time they climbed up into a shelf at the top of the kitchen, chewed their way through three layers of paper and plastic bags, and ate the whole thing. They also love toast, butter, baguettes, bacon, dog food, and anything else they can find. Of course, they love fish, tuna salad, crab cakes, and soft shells, as well as roast chicken and chicken soup with rice. They are the best!"

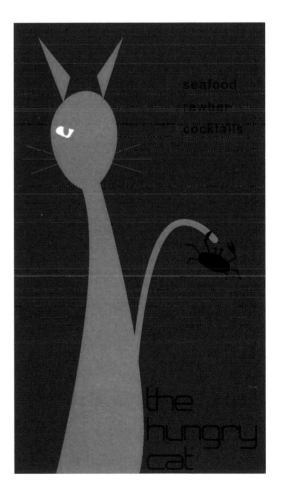

THE HUNGRY CAT'S CRAB CAKES

Los Angeles, CA

Yoda and Tweety Bird, the felines who live with star chefs Suzanne Goin and David Lentz, heartily approve of The Hungry Cat's delicious crab cake recipe. Here's how you can make this delicacy at home.

1 pound crabmeat
1 teaspoon Dijon mustard
1 teaspoon Worcestershire
   sauce
1 egg
½ cup mayonnaise

Juice of 1 lemon
1 cup crushed, unsalted Saltine
   crackers
¼ cup olive oil
Salt and pepper to taste

Preheat oven to 400°F. Pick through the crabmeat for shells. In a bowl, combine the mustard, Worcestershire sauce, egg, mayonnaise, and lemon juice. Add crabmeat to mixture. Add saltines and mix very gently; you want to keep the crabmeat as much together as possible. Form into cakes and refrigerate.

Shape the cakes into 4-ounce patties. Heat a large sauté pan over high heat for 2 minutes. Swirl in olive oil and sauté the cakes about 5 minutes until crispy (turn down the heat down if they are cooking too fast). Turn the cakes over and sauté a few more minutes and then (if you like) finish them in the oven for another 3 to 4 minutes.

NOTE: Felines often loathe the taste of citrus, so modify for finicky cats by omitting the lemon juice altogether.

MAKES SIX 4-OUNCE CAKES

TIP:

Even the hungriest cat would have a hard time finishing an entire crab cake by himself, so you'll have plenty left over. Don't fry up too many more cakes than you and your guests can eat!

THE SKINNY ON SKIN

Continuing the fishy theme, if you're having broiled fish for dinner, do save a small part of the skin as an offering for your cat. Whether it's seafood (salmon, for example) or freshwater fish (such as trout), your cat will be happy to accept. And the Omega-3s in the fish skin will do wonders for Kitty's skin, coat, and overall well-being, especially in the cold of winter.

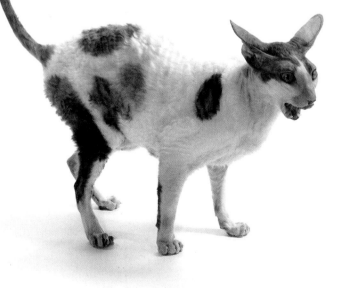

UP TO SNIFF

Since cooking for cats means using a fair amount of fish, make sure the atmosphere in your kitchen doesn't become overwhelmed with unpleasantly "fishy" odors. Airing the place out is always useful; you can also use the brilliant O*ZONELite anywhere a light bulb is needed—it's an energy-saving full-spectrum bulb that does double duty as an air purifier. Finally, if you like to keep things smelling nice by burning scented candles, be advised that paraffin ones emit toxic fumes that are harmful to pets and people. Opt for a fragrant soy candle instead. Just never leave a lit candle unattended in a home with cats.

THE MERE
SUGGESTION OF
GRILLED MEAT MAKES
SULLIVAN
THE MAINE COON'S
MOUTH WATER.

steak au poivre/ steak au naturel

Human gourmets can't resist a steak au poivre that's crusted with lots of freshly-ground black and white pepper, plus other spices. For our feline counterparts, however, it's best to hold the spices. Share a high-protein feast with your feline friend by preparing two identical steaks on an indoor grill. The sirloin at left is misted lightly with olive oil; the one at right is oiled. Then generously seasoned with pepper, coarse grains of sea-salt, and a dusting of aromatic nutmeg. (To keep things safely separate, we used a Foreman Double Knockout grill, pictured.)

steak au poivre/
steak au naturel

Pre-heat an indoor grill according to the manufacturer's directions. For the Steak au Poivre, mist with olive oil, then season liberally to taste with freshly-ground black, white, and/or pink peppercorns, coarse sea-salt, and freshly-grated nutmeg. For the Steak au Naturel, lightly moisten your choice of beef cut with olive oil using a mister.

Place on opposite sides of the grill, and cook until desired doneness is reached.

NOTE: Cats like steak rare, so please don't overcook!

LIKE THE REST
OF HER SPECIES,
BEAUJENNA
SIMPLY LOVES
RED MEAT.

BEAUJENNA

HAS A NOSE FOR FLAVOR
AND LIKES HER TURKEY
SOUPED UP WITH A DASH
OF DINNER PARTY
SEASONING.

TALKING TURKEY

Turkey is high on the list of meats that cats can't resist; I have yet to meet the cat who would pass up this dinner treat. One medium-size roast turkey can feed several cats for several days. The Meow Chow version is less of a production than the traditional Thanksgiving bird, because there's no stuffing inside the cavity to add to the roasting time or complicate carving.

If you don't mind that the turkey won't look picture-perfect as it emerges from the oven, then roast it breast-side down, so that the juices flow breastward, ensuring the tenderness of the white meat. And if you're certain that the fresh bird you're cooking was organically raised, try cutting off a raw wing before roasting—remove the meat and separate out the bones— and present the raw bones to Kitty as a chew toy. Like dogs, cats enjoy gnawing on raw meat bones to keep their teeth healthy.

Please serve only raw bones; don't ever give cooked bones to any pet. During cooking, bones become brittle and can easily splinter, puncturing the animal's intestines and resulting in fatal injury. Better safe than sorry: always go with raw.

roast Turkey

Preheat the oven to 350°F. Rub one fresh, organic turkey with olive oil. Place in a pan on a roasting rack and roast for about 35 minutes per pound of turkey. A medium to large turkey will serve several cats (and a few humans, too) with plenty enough for leftovers.

OPTIONAL: For a flavor boost, sprinkle a dash of Dinner Party seasoning in your cat's choice of salmon-, chicken-, or beef-flavor.

SASSY

CONTEMPLATES HER
BOWL IN HOPES THAT IT
WILL SOON OVERFLOW
WITH FRESHLY ROASTED
MEAT.

TOM'S CHICKEN SOUP

Tom, my pink-nosed gray tabby, is a cross between Puss in Boots and a linebacker. High on his list of favorite snacks, after freshly roasted turkey, is tender stewed chicken. (Don't tell Tom I told you, but he's missing two of his eye-teeth, so it's particularly convenient for him to savor this melt-in-your-mouth meat treat.) Enjoy the chicken broth yourself—it's especially warming on a winter day—and save the meat for your favorite feline carnivore. Just be sure you've removed all the tiny chicken bones before serving the meat to your cat.

1 whole chicken

5 stalks celery, untrimmed

5 carrots, untrimmed

Few sprigs parsley or dill

With a piece of string, tie the chicken in unbleached cheesecloth so that bones can't float all over the place. Place chicken, plus all other ingredients, in a large stockpot. Fill pot with filtered water to cover. Bring to a boil; lower heat, and simmer for 2 hours.

Remove chicken and debone; set meat aside. Reserve cartilage tips from bones as a nutritional treat: the cartilage contains glucosamine, which helps old, stiff feline joints to stay lubricated and working properly.

To spice things up for humans who like it hot, add paprika to the soup.

NOTE: To make the soup ultra-kid-friendly, boil fun-shaped noodles or orzo, not in water, but in a few cups of chicken broth, for the number of minutes specified on the package. The noodles will be unbelievably rich and delicious. (This was my favorite menu item as a youngster, and it's still my ultimate comfort food.)

SERVES FOUR PEOPLE AND TWO CATS, WITH PLENTY OF LEFTOVERS

snacks

Butter

. . . .

Catnip Salad

. . . .

Catnip Tea

. . . .

Green-eyed Greens

BUTTER THEM UP

You may notice your cat coveting the butter as it stands on the table alongside the jams, jellies, and other tea-time paraphernalia. A small pat of butter can go far in helping a cat with a hairball problem. Just for fun, spread a teaspoon of butter on the inside of the Kitty Kong (below), an ingenious rubber toy created for felines. Watch as Kitty works to get at the creamy treat!

But if you notice your cat experiencing gastro-intestinal upset (vomiting or diarrhea), itching, or runny eyes, he could be having an allergic reaction. In that case, bring him to the vet, and don't feed him dairy again.

NIP AND TUCK

Cats are definitely not vegetarians. They are, however, willing to approach a vegetable with serious interest if—and it's a big if!—the "vegetable" in question is a toy that contains generous amounts of pungent, dried catnip.

There's no better recipe for a good time than catnip, which brings out the frisky kitten in adult and even senior cats. When herbs are dried, they become more potent—compare the difference in taste between, say, dried basil and fresh. But fresh herbs have a lovely aroma and flavor, so whenever possible, treat your cat to a small green salad of fresh cat nip—she will love it. It's easy to grow your own (from seeds to sprouts takes about two weeks)—or ask at your local farmer's market.

A CARROT HOLDS
POLARA'S
ATTENTION ONLY
BECAUSE IT'S FILLED
WITH ORGANIC DRIED
CATNIP.

catnip tea

Cats take their catnip raw, but humans boil the leaves of this special mint to make a soothing tea. A natural digestant, mint is very helpful in calming an upset stomach.

2 or 3 catnip leaves
Boiling water

Put catnip leaves in a mug; pour boiling water over them. Steep for several minutes and enjoy.

NOTE: Eating the leaves also helps to calm stomach upset. In the warm months, simply pour over ice to make iced catnip tea.

Tea Time
with a Twist

In Japan, it's traditional to brew tea in a cast-iron teapot. For an update on this tradition, why not brew catnip leaves? While humans drink their catnip as tea, felines look forward to a leaf or two of fresh catnip.

Enjoy catnip tea in a mug from the "Meow" Fiesta collection by Betty Crocker. Max the Maine Coon (opposite) supervises the catnip tea ceremony.

FIELDS
LIKES A HEARTY NIBBLE
OF GRASS TO KEEP HIS
DIGESTIVE SYSTEM
IN TOP SHAPE.

Green-eyed Greens

—◗●◖—

One surefire recipe for a happy cat is to provide her with patches of fresh wheatgrass. Nibbling on the green stuff aids feline digestion, helps prevent hair balls, and imparts a healthy sheen to a cat's coat. That's why I always keep a generous pot of grass on hand for my cats' grazing pleasure. If you have a green thumb, it's a no-brainer to grow your own. Otherwise, inquire at your local farmer's market or health food store for boxes of fresh, organic wheatgrass.

And if you really want to pamper your puss, cut the ends off a few grass blades and combine them with a few leaves of cat mint to create a salad of mixed kitty greens! Also known as catnip, this mint in its fresh form is guaranteed to drive your cat wild with excitement. For added flourish, why not top the "salad" with a pinch of dried catnip?

Tips of about **5** grass leaves, ½-inch long

4 or **5** leaves cat mint
Pinch of dried catnip (optional)

Combine fresh greens on a plate or in a bowl; top with dried catnip.

SERVES ONE OR TWO CATS

75

special occasions

—————— ⊶ ——————

Aristocat Anchovies

· · · · · · · · ·

Sushi Picnic

· · · · · · · · ·

Easter Centerpiece

· · · · · · · · ·

Pushkin's Cashew Delight à la Mode

· · · · · · · · ·

Hazelnut Meringue Cat Tortes

aristocat anchovies

Regent Beverly Wilshire, Beverly Hills

Traveling felines who stay with their humans at posh hotels are likely to dine in on special room-service meals created expressly for their discerning palates. A highlight of the Pet Amenities menu at the famed Regent Beverly Wilshire is Aristocat Anchovies served in—what else?—a gleaming silver bowl. Cats can easily enjoy this treat at home (silver bowl optional).

1 can boneless anchovy filets in olive oil

1 sprig parsley, for garnish

Drain oil from fish thoroughly and blot on paper towels; arrange on plate. Garnish with sprig of parsley.

NOTE: Actress Halle Berry feeds her cat *boquerones*, a small, white variety of anchovy imported from Spain!

SERVES 2 TO 4 CATS

This deluxe cat bowl is hand-hammered from a solid silver ingot.

SUSHI PICNIC

If you've established that seafood agrees with your cat (please see previous pages), then try serving Kitty a tempting piece of salmon sashimi the next time you order in from your favorite Japanese restaurant. Other tempting options from the raw bar include tuna, squid, and sweet shrimp. And if you're dining out on sushi, remember to bring a "Kitty Bag" home for Puss. Obviously, a sushi picnic is not something you'll be having every day, but everyone deserves a fancy, indulgent treat once in a while!

Remember, quality really counts with raw fish, for felines as well as humans. Be sure to patronize only restaurants with a reputation for serving the freshest, highest-grade sushi. Remember, too, that cats should not eat the green horseradish known as wasabi, so always specify "no wasabi" when you place your sushi order, and hold the soy sauce (too much sodium is bad for cats).

SPLENDOR IN THE GRASS

Fresh wheatgrass makes a lovely home accent—it's safe for felines to nibble on and doubles as a festive centerpiece. Nothing's more stylish than edible greenery! Framed by a simple wooden box, wheatgrass is especially perfect at Easter; simply scatter decorated Easter eggs across it, or prop them up in between the leaves of grass.

On the subject of felines and flora, please don't display any type of lily, cut or potted, in a home with cats—not even on special occasions. Lilies are a recipe for disaster, as the beautiful, trumpet-shaped blooms are deadly to felines. Cats find themselves attracted by the flowers' fragrant aroma to approach and take a nibble. And if any part of the plant is ingested, the toxic substances damage the cat's kidneys, which leads to kidney failure and death. If you suspect your cat may have chewed on a lily, run, don't walk, to the emergency animal hospital. If you're planning to bring the gift of flowers to a friend's home for Easter or Passover, but you're not sure whether or not they have a pet feline, always opt for a bouquet with no lilies. Safety first!

CANDY

THE SIAMESE AGREES
THAT A PLAIN WOODEN
BOX OF GRASS
MAKES A LOVELY
CENTERPIECE.

PUSHKIN'S CASHEW DELIGHT À LA MODE

— ⟩●⟨ —

Cats really shouldn't partake of dessert, as too much sugar is not good for their health. However, considering felines' love of creamy things, why not give them the opportunity to enjoy a tiny amount of ice cream the next time you're enjoying this delicious frozen treat? It's safe so long as the flavor is anything other than chocolate, with no chocolate chips or swirls.

Scoop one teaspoon of vanilla ice cream or gelato, then top with ½ teaspoon of organic cashew butter. Serve—and watch how fast it disappears. If your cat is not crazy for cashew butter, make it a sweet-savory morsel by substituting a few bonito flakes as an ice-cream garnish instead!

JASMINE
THE KITTEN NAVIGATES
AROUND A PAPER DOILY
WITH THE POISE FOR
WHICH CATS ARE
RENOWNED.

Hazelnut Meringue
Cat Tortes

The talented Seen Lippert cooked at California's famed Chez Panisse before becoming the chef at New York City's Across the Street and, later, helping to develop Yale University's Sustainable Food Project. She has four cats, Miel (Spanish for Honey), Macy, Miles, and Mimi. That means a lot of empty cat-food cans. For Seen, both at work and at home, an awareness of the environment and keeping it clean and green is key. So she does her part by repurposing empty cat-food cans as bakeware! Read on to find out how.

¾ cup plus 2 tablespoons
 hazelnuts
1 cup granulated sugar
1 tablespoon cornstarch

6 egg whites
Very small pinch of salt
Powdered sugar for dusting

Ten empty 5½-ounce cat food cans, or twelve empty 3-ounce cans, thoroughly cleaned and scalded, tops and bottoms removed with a can opener (alternately, use store-bought ring molds).

Preheat oven to 350°F. Put the hazelnuts on a baking sheet and toast them in the oven for 8 minutes. Remove from oven and put the nuts into a sieve. Rub vigorously to remove as much of the outside skin as possible. Allow nuts to cool completely. Put the nuts, sugar, and cornstarch into the bowl of a food processor and pulse mixture until finely ground. Prepare torte molds by buttering and flouring the inside of the cleaned cat-food cans. Place molds onto a baking sheet lined with parchment paper or a silpat.

Put the egg whites into a mixing bowl and whip until glossy and just firm enough to hold a peak when you remove whip (or hand-held beaters) from bowl. Fold egg whites into the nut mixture and stir until just blended. Put batter into prepared torte molds, filling them just to the top of the ring. Put in oven and bake for 15 minutes. The cakes should be just firm and springy. If not, put back in oven for 5 more minutes.

Allow to cool, then run a knife around the inside of the mold to release the torte. Using a spatula, remove tortes from baking paper and serve with a generous dusting of powdered sugar or your favorite frosting.

MAKES 10 TORTES

JACK
THE TUXEDO CAT IS
PERMANENTLY DRESSED
FOR ANY SPECIAL
OCCASION.

CHOCOLATE alert

Cats must never eat chocolate, as the theobromine in the cocoa causes a toxic reaction. Dark or baker's chocolate is especially toxic, as it contains higher levels of theobromine, so be especially careful to close your curious cat out of the kitchen when cooking or baking with chocolate. (If you suspect that your cat may have ingested chocolate, no matter what color, rush him to the emergency veterinary hospital without delay.) The only way that cats and chocolate can safely mix is in this adorable feline mold, enrobed in white chocolate, created by the brilliant Belgian chocolatier Martine's Chocolates.

STYLISH DINING
accessories

This is not a matter of snobbery: Cheap, low-grade plastic imparts an off putting taste to whatever it comes in contact with. Some cats won't even touch food or water if it's been "tainted" by plastic, and that kind of abstinence ultimately leads to serious health problems. So serving your cat with designer food bowls could actually help extend her life.

And, just for fun, serve a cat's food in bowls that come in lovely fashion colors, including a range of watery blues. If your cat has blue eyes, match them to the color of her bowls!

MATCHING
**SIMON BLUE
EYES'S**
PEEPERS TO A BLUE
BOWL IS A
NO-BRAINER.

served WITH Love

For a cat, what he eats on is just as important as what he eats. Tableware is much more than an accessory; it's the first step to a healthy cat meal. Cheap plastic bowls are simply not acceptable. Only high-quality plastic or resin dishes may be used for felines.

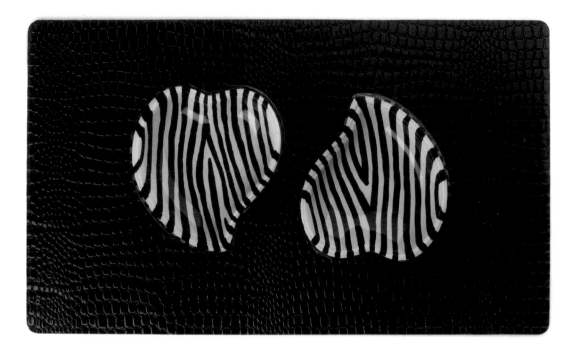

High-quality plastic bowls by Cats Rule, in a stunning zebra stripe, bring fashionable sophistication to the feline dining experience. Underneath them is a vinyl placemat that's as stylish as it is easy to wipe clean.

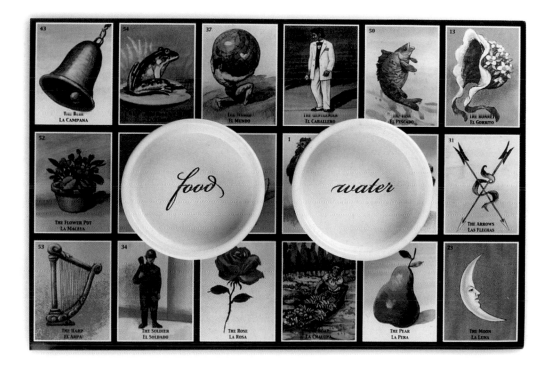

Bringing the elegance of dining out to everyday meals at home, white ceramic bowls by Harry Barker pop against the brilliant colors of a "Loteria" placemat designed by Zarela Martinez, of New York City's world-renowned Zarela's Restaurant.

YELLOW PLATE SPECIAL

Metal and ceramic bowls are the safest bet for serving forth feline feasts. Of course, if you insist on posh feline tableware, there are many attractive options, including Fiesta bowls emblazoned with the legend HERE KITTY KITTY . . .

When setting your own table, might as well use simple, sturdy tableware that celebrates the concept of sharing: vitrified-china plates by Homer Laughlin, makers of Fiesta, proudly telegraph the words MEOW CHOW!

What goes in must come out, and the quality of a cat's stool is an excellent indicator of wellness. Green tea is a delicious beverage that also happens to be effective in preventing cancer—but it's not for cats' consumption, as it contains high levels of caffeine (bad for felines). However, green tea does have natural anti-bacterial qualities thanks to a chemical compound called Catechin. For some time, drinkers of green tea have been known to re-use the brewed leaves by drying them and scattering them in the cat-box to absorb odors. Now there's even a brand of cat litter called Green Tea Leaves. Made of—you guessed it—green tea leaves, it marks the purr-fect end to a *Meow Chow* meal.

FELINE DESIGN

Creatures of ultimate refinement, cats always insist on the finest in everything. Case in point: a Bengal kitty named June admiring her reflection as she enjoys a meal atop a highly-polished antique—a painted table by the French furniture designer André Arbus. The plate that holds this fabulous feline's food is nothing less than Tiffany china!

When arranging flowers with cats, choose anything but lilies. These faux gardenias are convincing and safe.

resource GUIDe

PAGE 3: "Meow Chow" plate available at Sylvester & Co., Sag Harbor, NY, 631-725-5012

PAGE 10: Heart-shaped "Mimi's Bowl" from Cats Rule, available at Petco stores, *www.petco.com*; for more stores, visit *www.catsrule.com* ; For information on Tom Cat Bakery, call 718-786-7659 or visit *www.tomcat-bakery.com*

PAGE 11: For information on Purina HA, available by prescription, ask your veterinarian or visit *www.purina.com* ; Cat food storage canister and scoop from Harry Barker, 800-444-2779 or *www.harrybarker.com*

PAGES 12–13: Curly Sue the Cornish Rex is pictured dining on an organic raw diet from K.E. Rush & Sons, 215-412-4110 or *www.natures-intent.com*. If you decide to feed your cat a raw diet, make sure that the meat is fresh and comes from a reputable source.

PAGE 14: Custom-built cat shelves to order from master carpenter Christopher Bailey; for information, email *baileychris@earthlink.net*. Because cats sometimes like to throw their food out of their bowl while eating, then lick it up, I made sure to coat the shelves with Pristine Eco Spec Interior Latex by Benjamin Moore, a paint used in hospitals. It's safer— and more pleasant—to use because it doesn't have the odor of conventional paints that contain Volatile Organic Compounds (VOCs). When decorating with hungry pets in mind, never use a flat finish paint, as it's impossible to keep clean; always opt for a finish that's easy to wipe down, such as

Benjamin Moore's Eggshell Enamel. For stores that carry Pristine Eco Spec, visit *www.benjaminmoore.com*

NOTE: Hungry cats sometimes present decorating challenges. Here's a feline-design tip: If you live with an elderly or ailing cat, or one with a habit of vomiting frequently, consider creative uses for clear vinyl. In my animal house, I had slipcovers made, then stuffed them with colorful Jiffy Thick & Quick yarn by Lion Brand (*www.lionbrand.com*). I even applied the same concept to a pair of antique shield-back side chairs, complete with brass nail heads! They're a cinch to wipe clean in the event of an "accident." The best custom clear vinyl slip covers are made by J&P Decorators, Long Island City, NY, 718-482-8500.

PAGE 16: Fiesta "Move Over Rover, Kitty's Taking Over" bowl available at Sylvester & Co., Sag Harbor, NY, 631-725-5012.

PAGE 17: Cat treats and loose catnip by Harry Barker, *www.harrybarker.com*

PAGE 20: My favorite moisturizer is Very Emollient Body Lotion by Alba Botanica; I know that it contains nothing that could harm my cats when they lick it off my hands and elbows! What's more, the company does not test products or ingredients on animals, nor do they ask others to do so for them. For stores, visit *www.albabotanica.com;*

Animal Allergy and Dermatology Specialists, NYC, 212-206-0969 or *www.animalallergyandderm.com*

PAGE 21: For information on Fage yogurt, visit *www.fageusa.com*

PAGE 24: For stores carrying my cats' favorite brand of kefir, Lifeway, call 847-967-1010 or visit *www.lifeway.net*

PAGE 27: "Fanny's Bowl" (silver tone) by Cats Rule, *www.catsrule.com*

PAGE 28: Oil mister by Bodum available at *www.bodum.com*

PAGE 29: Cat food storage canister by Harry Barker, 800-444-2779 or *www.harrybarker.com*

PAGE 40: Pink and blue metal rubber-ringed bowls by Prima Pet (also available in orange, red, yellow, and two shades of green) from Fetch, *www.fetchpets.com* ; for more stores, *visit www.primapet.com*

PAGE 41: To make tartar sauce, simply combine equal spoonfuls sweet pickle relish (my favorite brand is B&G Foods, *www.bgfoods.com*) and mayonnaise. Or, finely chop a dill pickle and half a red pepper, seeded and finely diced, and combine with about 3 tablespoons mayonnaise.

PAGE 42: For information on the Brita water filtration system, call 800-24-BRITA or visit *www.brita.com ;* "Coco's Bowl" by Cats Rule, *www.catsrule.com*

PAGE 48: The Hungry Cat, Hollywood, CA, 323-462-2155; books by M.F.K. Fisher and Ruth Reichl available at Kitchen Arts & Letters, NYC, 212-876-5550

PAGE 53: To order O*ZoneLite bulbs, call 800-494-8292 or visit *www.ozonelite.com;* For stores that carry "O Christmas Tree" soy candle by Ergo, call 214-905-9050 or visit *www.ergo-candles.com*

PAGE 55: Foreman Double Knockout Grill from Macy's, *www.macys.com*; for more stores, visit *www.esalton.com*

PAGE 58: "Fanny's Bowl" (silver tone) by Cats Rule, *www.catsrule.com*

PAGE 59: Dinner Party seasoning by Halo, Purely for Pets available at Pet Stop, 212-580-2400 or *www.petstopnyc.com* (for more stores, call 800-426-4256 or visit *www.halopets.com*)

PAGE 60: Free-range turkey from Quattro's Game Farm, Pleasant Valley, NY, 845-635-8202

PAGE 61: "Josie's Bowl" (faux tortoise) by Cats Rule, *www.catsrule.com*

PAGE 67: Kitty Kong and other Kong products available at Petco stores, *www.petco.com*; for more stores, call 303-216-2626 or visit *www.kongcompany.com*

PAGE 68: Fresh, organic catnip from Windfall Farms, Montgomery, NY, 845-457-5988

PAGE 69: "Curious Cat" carrot-shaped organic catnip toy (also available in other veggie shapes) from Castor & Pollux Pet Works, 800-875-7518 or visit *www.castorpolluxpet.com*

Curious Cat catnip toys by Castor &
Pollux, www.castorpolluxpet.com.

PAGE **72**: For information on Betty Crocker "Meow" special-edition Fiesta, call 800-432-4959 or visit *www.bettycrocker.com*

PAGE **73**: Cast-iron teapot from Katagiri, NYC, 212-755-3566 or *www.katagiri.com*

PAGE **74**: Organic wheatgrass in terracotta pot from Greener Pastures, Brooklyn, NY, 718-852-3979 or *www.grassworksnyc.com*

PAGE **78**: Regent Beverly Wilshire, 310-275-5200 or *www.fourseasons.com*

PAGE **79**: To order solid silver cat bowl, email *sheila.parness@parness.com*

PAGE **80**: Salmon sushi from Blue Ribbon Sushi, NYC, 212-343-0404

PAGE **83**: Organic wheatgrass in wood box from Greener Pastures, 718-852-3979 or *www.grassworksnyc.com*

PAGE **84**: For stores that carry Maranatha cashew butter (our cover cat's favorite), call 510-346-3860 or visit *www.maranathanutbutters.com;* My favorite vanilla gelato is from Il Laboratorio del Gelato, NYC, 212-343-9922 or *www.laboratoriodelgelato.com*

PAGE **85**: Paper doily from New York Cake Supplies, 800-942-2539, *www.nycake.com*

PAGE **86**: To learn more about the Yale Sustainable Food Project, visit *www.yale.edu/sustainablefood*

PAGE **89**: Chocolate cat from Martine's Chocolates, NYC, 212-744-6289 or *www.martineschocolates.com*

PAGES **92–93**: When washing cats' dishes, always take care to use a gentle, environmentally friendly dishwashing liquid such as Ecover, *www.ecover.com;* Bowls and Serve it Up Dual-Ended Food Spoons by Cats Rule available at Petco, *www.petco.com;* for more stores, visit *www.catsrule.com*

PAGE **94**: Zebra-striped "Coco's Bowl" and black vinyl faux-crocodile food mat from Cats Rule, *www.catsrule.com*

PAGE **95**: Zarela Mexican-style "Loteria" placemat, designed by chef Zarela Martinez for Town & Country Linen,

available at Wal-Mart stores, *www.walmart.com* (for more stores, call 800-870-7911). White "Food" and "Water" bowls by Harry Barker, 800-444-2779 or *www.harrybarker.com*

PAGE 96: Fiesta "Here Kitty Kitty" bowl in Sunflower and Homer Laughlin "Meow Chow" plate from Sylvester & Co., Sag Harbor, NY, 631-725-5012

PAGE 97: To order Green Tea Leaves cat litter, visit *www.nextgenpet.com*; "Charlie's Box" from Cats Rule available at Petco stores, *www.petco.com*; for more stores, visit *www.catsrule.com*

PAGE 112: "Reserved" sign from Chef Restaurant Supply (where a sweet tabby cat patrols the premises), NYC, 212-254-6714

School of cotton fish placemats by Luxury Kitten from Paw & Chic, 866-995-9161 or www.pawandchic.com

acknowledgments

———— ▶● ————

THE AUTHOR EXTENDS HEARTFELT THANKS TO THE FOLLOWING, WITHOUT
WHOM THIS BOOK WOULD NOT HAVE BEEN POSSIBLE:

*Project Editor Sandra Gilbert, Zaro Weil, Ljiljana Baird,
Sarah Rainwater, Tomoko Shimura, George and Martha Szabo,
Todd Oldham, Christian Erhard of Leica Camera, Suzanne Goin,
Seen Lippert, Ruth Reichl, Susan Richmond, Anne Marie Karash
and everyone at the Humane Society of New York,
Dr. Heather Peikes, Christine Butler, Shannon Reed,
Charlotte Barnard, Randi Hoffman and everyone at Bide-a-Wee,
Andorra Luciano and Jen Ebert, RuthAnne Miller,
NYC Siamese Rescue (www.nycsiamese.com) and
Marie Morreale, with special thanks to John Maher.*

TREATS ARE IN ORDER FOR OUR YOUNG HUMAN MODELS, MELINA MCGAW
AND JACK WALSH, AS WELL AS ALL THE CATS WHO MODELED FOR THE
PHOTOGRAPHS—THEY ARE, IN ORDER OF APPEARANCE:

*Pushkin, Smokey, Jasmine, Hannah, Curly Sue, Ninotchka,
Ludmilla, Candy, Jack, Cap'n Andy, Scaredy, Cyrus, Charlie,
Sullivan, Beaujenna, Sassy, PeeWee, Polara, Max, Fields,
Simon Blue Eyes, June, Priscilla, and Zoolander Bowie.*